Title

Applause for British "Fairness and Justice"
An Illusionary Paradise

Copyright

Ipemndoh *dan Iyan* © 2012/2013
ba(goodhons-socsci)adv.dip(crim)cert(priresh)mphil(pol&ir)

2

Dedication

To the redoubtable God I dedicate this work for the Lord is my Guide and Guardian who surrounds me with Grace, Prosperity and Righteousness. I thank God for the Gift of Confidence imbued in me, and the Peace enveloping me thus, even in adversity. I value God for the Fearlessness with which I Delight in life because the Lord is with me at all times and always Comforting me. I am forever Grateful to God for allowing me the Joy of living and Glory everlasting. I Bathe under the Lord's Showers of Goodness and Mercy as I am Elevated above those who seek to injure me. I am Proud in my acceptance of belonging to God and Happy in knowing that the Lord is for, and at, all times my Sanctuary. I love the Lord God without Restraint for Never putting me in Want in the Periods in which I Lack.©2009/2012/2013

I owe my secondary dedication to that younger Occidental ('White') British male who boasted to me that the British are "known for fairness and justice" on that day in January 2012. Or did you say "known for justice and fairness"? Never mind, you were my immediate inspiration for this essay. Thank you.

Preface

This essay started as an argument on both the **misconception** of *justice* for *fairness*, and the British claim to be "fair and just". The part of the essay undertaking the thesis on *justice* as *fairness* became quite involved. After much deliberation it became clear that the thesis on *just/justice* as *fair/fairness* needed to be treated on its own.

Quite apart from the justification that *just/justice* as *fair/fairness* had to be engaged solely, it was also obvious that the British claim to be "fair and just" had a **peculiarity** that equally called for a *distinct* discussion. Ordinarily, the claim presumes *fair* as *interchangeable* with *just* in intent. However, the presumption of *fair* meaning *just* is *manifestly* misguided. The misguidance that is, in fact, an *illogicality* has been traced to Aristotle and his *Nicomachean Ethics* written around 350 BCE. In attributing this *infantile* logic to Aristotle, his *important* mind was and is placed in much *disrepute* before those, who can ordinarily discern the **nonsense** of *just* as meaning *fair* but, who do not care to read Aristotle directly themselves. In *Nicomachean Ethics*, Aristotle, in fact, believed *fair/fairness* to be one part of *just/justice* with *lawful* making up the other part. For Aristotle, *just/justice* is the *bigger* picture and *fair/fairness* is a *smaller* image. However, in *Politics*, Aristotle appears to be defining *justice* as a *process of making judgements* but still including *law* as a part of *justice*. Aristotle's *Politics* does not coincide fully with Aristotle's *Nicomachean Ethics* on Aristotle's understanding of *justice*. *Politics*, in particular, was unable to *isolate* the conception of *justice* from *justice* the process. This lack of refinement in Aristotle's thinking could lead to *confusion of mind* with those who either did not read both of his theses *closely* or are simply *regurgitating* what previous writers wrote of their understanding of Aristotle on *fairness* and *justice*.

Thus, when the British people say they are "fair and just" they are *primarily* being *tautologous* in expression and *confused* of mind. These *strays* of logic are evident in the *inability* to separate *fair* from *just* in any attempted explanation. It would suffice, therefore, for them to simply say they are *just* and one would understand that they are claiming to be both *fair* and *lawful* in accordance with Aristotle's thinking in *Nicomachean Ethics*. More important than the *mistaken* understanding of Aristotle's *fairness* and *justice*, however, is whether when we hear the *cliché* of "fair and just" we are merely listening to repetitive **defend rhetoric** or being enlightened by what the British believe to be **truism**. It is this question of *defend rhetoric* **or** *truism* that the essay tackles with an interrogation of the laws and practices of the British State. The interrogation in turn is set against the British system of governance which consists of five traditions made up of seven practices.

Abstract

When the British say they are "fair and just", the query immediately to mind is whether we are merely hearing repetitive defend rhetoric or are being enlightened by some **self-assurance** that the British not only believe what they say but can also **evidence** this self-assurance that they claim. Intellectually, the self-assurance boasts two separate qualities; *fair* and *just* notwithstanding the universal consensual assumption that the two represent the same value (yet are expressed in tautology). *Fairness* – from which *fair* emerged as both an adjective and a verb – is an **inherent** quality of the human being. The quality is innate in the human being. Justice – from which *just* emerged as both an adjective and a verb – on the other hand is mechanism designed by the human mind, to all intents and purposes, to deliver *fairness*.

This essay responds to the *question* of British *fairness* and *justice* by exploring the laws and practices of the British territorial-State. This is a necessary tack because in order to understand how *fair* and *just* a population is, the appropriate unit of analysis is the **impersonal** level of the State on a plain that enables us to review the country's laws and Governmental practices. In undertaking this exercise in this manner, the essay works with the British *socio-political process* as the *over-arching benchmark*. The essay, therefore, examines British *fairness* within the following activities of the State; (i) criminal law, (ii) employment law, (iii) social policy as an aspect of the law, (iv) property law, (v) discretionary power to 'State Apparatuses', and (vi) the five traditions of governance made up of seven practices comprising (i) three types of **democracy**, (ii) a **constitutional monarchy**, (iii) a **parliamentary oligarchy**, (iv) an **hereditary nobility** and (v) a **lifetime nobility**.

This essay concludes that the British *claim* of custodianship to *fairness* is not **intellectually** sound and is founded on **false applause**. It is at best a *boast* premised on "*unconscious falsehood*". As a **utility**, it is an *ideological rhetoric* and as ideologies go, they are either *credible* or *incredulous*.

Contents

Introduction

Sometime in January 2012 I was in conversation with an Occidental ('White') Briton. He asked me where I came from "*originally*" and I responded with "that place called Nigeria." "Why," he asked, "do you say that place called Nigeria?" I replied with the answer that "the country is the *most-artificial* of countries. It was *manufactured* by the British colonial master." "Surely," he persisted, "you must be proud to be Nigerian. I am proud to be British." Interesting, I thought; he is *not* seeing me as "British" against the possibility that he was a toddler when I arrived in the United Kingdom (UK). I then asked him what being "British" meant reminding him that the '*hailing*' of "British" comprises the main *ethnic compositions* of **English**, **Northern Irish**, **Scottish** and **Welsh**. My fellow interlocutor *failed* to articulate any **homogeneity** of the *English*, the *Northern Irish*, the *Scottish* and the *Welsh*. He ventured eventually to submit that being "British" is *synonymous* with *fairness* and *justice*. Notice the *ridiculous* jump from a *geo-social* description of "British" to a *metaphysical* attributions of *just/justice* and *fair/fairness*. I did not pull him up on the *anomaly* of the jump from a geo-social *identity* to a philosophical *pseudo-argument*. Nor did I challenge him on the *fairness* and *justice* **hype**.

The claim of being "fair and just" ordinarily follows the *presumption* of *fair* as *interchangeable* with *just* in intent and it is, therefore, tautologous in expression. The logic of the presumption is **unsound**. Unknown to him, that younger man inspired me to *question* the common British *enthusiastic* **self-proclamation** of being "fair and just" and to *intellectually* challenge the **consensual** *misconception* of *justice* as meaning *fairness*.

I am going to use these pages, *firstly*, to set the scene regarding what can *rationally* be understood as *fair/fairness* on the one hand and *just/justice* on the other. *Secondly*, the essay will *interrogate* the *assumed* homogeneity of the "British" people. *Thirdly*, I will *explore* British *sense of fairness* and British *application of justice* on the ground by looking at British laws and implementation in general and social policies in particular in examining *fairness* and *justice* as these principles apply within the British **socio-political** environment. This third aspect of the essay is set against the background of whether when a British person says s/he is "fair and just", we are merely hearing **repetitive defend rhetoric**[i] or we are being reminded of what that British individual believes to be **truism**.

Acknowledging *Fairness*; Rationalizing *Justice*

The **unsound** logic of misconceiving *justice* for *fairness* has been *traced* to Aristotle and this misconception had become *universally* **consensual**. In attributing the misconception to Aristotle he has been rendered a great disservice. Aristotle never interchanged *fair* with *just* or *fairness* with *justice*. Aristotle, in fact, believed *fair/fairness* to be one part of *just/justice* with *lawful* making up the other part. Aristotle submitted in his **Nicomachean Ethics** that "The unjust has been divided into the unlawful and the unfair, and the **just** into the **lawful** and the **fair**. ..."[ii] It has to be noted, however, that in **Politics**, Aristotle seems to be defining *justice* as a *process of making judgements* but still including *law* as a part of *justice*. Aristotle's *Politics* does not coincide fully with Aristotle's *Nicomachean Ethics* on Aristotle's understanding of *justice*. *Politics*, in particular, was unable to *isolate* the conception of *justice* from *justice* the process. This lack of refinement in Aristotle's thinking could lead to *confusion of mind* with his readers. To fully grasp Aristotle's discussions on *fairness* and *justice* we have to read very closely both his *Nicomachean Ethics*, and *Politics*.

Notwithstanding my challenge of the **distortion** of Aristotle's logics regarding *fairness* and *justice*, I do not agree with Aristotle, himself, that *fair/fairness* is a sub-division of *just/justice* as he claimed in *Nicomachean Ethics*. This essay acknowledges *fair/fairness* as a *natural* quality of the human being and *latent transactional* expectation between humans. On the other hand, the essay recognises *just/justice* as the *structured mechanism* with which Government manages relations between entities within society whether or not these entities are individuals or a collective of individuals or organizations of a collective of organizations.

In making the distinction between *fair/fairness* and *just/justice*, the essay takes illumination from a well-known figure worldwide. This figure is Jesus the Christ who is recognised primarily as "the son of God" or "the personification of God" or "the messenger of Allah." He could also be identified, by those who care to do so, as one of the greatest philosophers the world has known. Although I can be usefully refer to as a Judaeo-Christian, I make reference in this work to Jesus the Christ not in any religious attribution. I rely here on Jesus the Christ for his accomplishments as a philosopher. To assist us with the concept of *fair/fairness* we take note of his injunction of "love thy neighbour as thyself" in Matthew 22:39. He was reminding us of God's commandment in Leviticus 19:17 that says "… you shall love thy neighbour as thyself". Neither the Bible nor Jesus the Christ was the first to illuminate *fair/fairness*. Centuries before the Bible, Ceng Zi, student to Confucius, introspected on whether in his "… interactions with friends [he had been] untrustworthy" and Zi Gong, a fellow student observed that "What [he did not] want done to [him, he would not] want to do to others".[iii] From his advice of "give unto Caesar what is Caesar's" in Mark 12:17, Jesus the Christ gave us an understanding of *just/justice*. He was illustrating that the *status quo* should be complied with. *Justice* for Jesus the Christ was the *practical process*. It was not a necessary question whether or not that process encompassed *fair/fairness*. Caesar was "the [earthly] power that be" and could *enforce* his demands. If Jesus the Christ was concerned with *justice* as *fairness* he would have reminded his audience that since God owns the earth, Caesar had no *stake* and no *right* to make demands of the populace.

Previously to Aristotle and Jesus the Christ, Socrates had tried to explain *justice* albeit unsuccessfully. Thrasymachus, in the exchange with Socrates in Plato's **Republic** over how to identify *justice*, argued that "… justice is nothing else than the interest of the stronger. … different forms of government make laws democratical, aristocratical, tyrannical, with a view to their several interests; and these laws, which are made by them for their own interests, are the justice which they deliver to their subjects, and him who transgresses them they punish as a breaker of the law, and unjust".[iv] Socrates did not agree with him and was *categorical* that "… there is no one in any rule who, in so far as he is a ruler, considers or enjoins what is for his own interest, but always what is for the interest of his subject …".[v] In his further expatiation of *justice* Thrasymachus posited that "… when there is an income-tax, the just man will pay more and the unjust less on the same amount of income; and when there is anything to be received the one gains nothing and the other much. …".[vi] We observe Thrasymachus' "the stronger" in our today's 'the *powerful* avoiding paying the correct taxes and/or bilking the State. The debate between Socrates and Thrasymachus over *justice* was a protracted one with Socrates essentially *chasing the tail*. Thrasymachus' *general exposition* on *justice* sustains even today notwithstanding Thrasymachus' own *ill-thought* attempt to frustrate his exposition of *justice* as *all-embracing*.

Who are the British People?

It is apparent from my introduction to this work that I do not accept the notion of the 'British' people as a societal *hermetic* populace. The "British People" are not a **monolith**. The "British People" are not even **unilingual**, that is to say, the *British People* do not have a *unitary* language. The *British People* are four **main** peoples, four nations, in a State. The *British People* also include peoples like myself; *recently originating* from Africa and others from Australasia, Asia, the Americas, Continental Europe, Eastern Europe, *et cetera*. So, in addition to the four main nations we have other nations from other continents (and sub-continents) making up the *British People*. As *erroneously* believed, Britain is not a 'Nation-State', as with most other countries in the world are not *Nation-States*.

The 'State' or the 'territorial-State' comprises (i) a geographical boundary of political sovereignty and, (ii) a **medley** of peoples across the Races pledging allegiance to that political sovereignty, and within which they conduct their civil, economic, political, and social interactions. The 'Nation' on the other hand presupposes primordial or near-primordial belongingness of **cultural** norms. These norms are shared **belief** systems complemented by common traditional practices. Those common **traditional** practices would normally be described as **customs**. The Nation can be argued sustainably as **shared** belongingness that cuts across *ordinary* geographical boundaries or territorial-State boundaries, and even Race. Thus, we can have a multiplicity of Races *constituting* a Nation or Nations and have members of a Nation spread across many territorial–States. Similarly, we can have more than one Nation making up a State. Nation or Nationhood is *begotten* from the *synthesis* of varying primordial or near-primordial values.

My formulation of the Nation is not to espouse the 'acculturation' or 'culture contact' thesis. By defining Nation/Nationhood as the synthesis of varying primordial or near-primordial values I argue neither the *subsumption* of one culture by another nor the transformation of all existing cultures into one new whole. My proposition is rather one of cultural *integration* with each diverse cultural contribution intact. These contributing cultures *continue* to be adhered to within their *respective spheres* outside the National identity but *without* interfering with the National Identity. This might be read as 'cultural fusion' but it is one where no culture is subordinate to another, at least in the psyches of the contributing cultures to the National Identity.

In arguing that the *hailing* of 'British' signifies the main *ethnicities* of **English**, **Northern Irish**, **Scottish** and **Welsh**, I have borrowed the conception of "hailing" from the French Philosopher, Louis Althusser. Althusser had made certain *contributions* to the *seminal* work from Valentin Nikolaevich Voloshinov, the Russian linguist, who had identified the **connection** between ideology and language. Voloshinov had submitted as follows; "*Without signs there is no ideology* ... any physical body may be perceived as an image. ... Any such artistic-symbolic image to which a particular physical object gives rise is already an ideological product. The physical object is converted into a sign".[vii] Althusser *explained* Voloshinov's thinking with the proposition that "*all ideology hails or interpellates concrete individuals as concrete subjects*, by the functioning of the category of the subject. ... ideology 'acts' or 'functions' in such a way that it 'recruits' subjects among the individuals (it recruits them all), or 'transforms' the individuals into subjects (it transforms them all) by that very precise operation which I have called *interpellation* or hailing, and which can be imagined along the lines of the most commonplace everyday police (or **other**) hailing: 'hey, you there!'".[viii] Thus, initially as *conceived* by Voloshinov and later as *elaborated* by Althusser, to say the *British* are *fair* and *just* is to **express** an **ideology**.

My following discussion, however, will borrow the expression *British* in collective description of the four nations of the British Isles because of their essentially shared **laws** and **formal practices**. This borrowing embraces the many other ethnicities comprised within the four main ethnicities. Where applicable, I will *differentiate*

Scottish law from the laws of the other national regions of the UK. My contention with the British *fairness* and *justice* **boast** is restricted to my exploration of the *law*, and **social policy**. I might also touch on moral questions impacting on the law and social policy because in addition to **enactments**, there are the **moral** etiquette and the **social** etiquette instructing statute and social policy, and the conduct of members of society (any society).

British Fairness in Criminal Law

Until the *Criminal Justice Act (CJA) 2003* the English, Northern Irish and Welsh jurisdictions of the UK were **bastions** of **juridical unfairness** to victims of crime even of crimes as heinous as murder. The "double jeopardy" technicality *entrenched* this juridical unfairness by ensuring that a suspect was not tried more than once for the same offence even if new evidence surfaced, except in instances of mistrial. The law that enshrined this *double jeopardy* **escape route** for suspects was part of the process of *justice*. The fact that this escape route in law was repealed is a *self-damning* recognition that it was not a *fair* implement even though it was part of the *justice* machinery for eon. The *CJA 2003* was the eventual *consequence* of the racist murder of Stephen Lawrence in South London. Lawrence was an African-Caribbean of eighteen (18) years and studying to become an architect at the time his life was **brutally** cut short in 1993. However, during the double jeopardy era, contrary to public understanding, *justice* was always served on both the *indicted* and the *victim* because "justice" is the administration of the law, the juridical process. *Justice* is "due process". It was not until the *Double Jeopardy (Scotland) Act (DJSA) 2011* that Scotland joined the rest of Britain in repealing the double jeopardy instrument of the law, of *justice*. The time lag in the jettisoning of the *double jeopardy* law between Scotland and the rest of the UK shows how wrong, **dead** wrong, my proud Occidental British interlocutor was with, and in, his *implied* belief in the homogenous condition of the British peoples.

British Fairness in Employment Law

The employment *arena* is still a **depository** of **unfairness** in British society. The employment *field*, in any society, is where the **greatest good** or the **worst harm** is done to the person. It is the one *theatre* in life with the opportunity for an individual to structure own and family's lifestyle with reasonable confidence because it provides the individual with the financial means to do so. It is the *battleground* of the livelihood one can be *proud* of. It is here too, that we find **substantial** evidence of the British **antithesis** to the philosophy of *fairness*.

If a *wronged* employee seeks redress in British courts s/he has three pathways. One pathway is the Employment Tribunal (ET). This pathway is *time-limited* to *three* months for the aggrieved employee to file a claim against a *particular* employer conduct otherwise that employee *forfeits* the opportunity to use this pathway. This British three months' time limit is held in *stark relief* against the **six** months' time limit in **Ireland**. So, here already compared with its next door neighbour, we find the British boast of being *fair* 'falling flat on its face'. Prior to the Cameron/Clegg Government there was no fee involved in pursuing this avenue but with the incumbency of this Government, the jury is only just sitting as to whether or not it would be as expensive to use as the other pathways. The Cameron/Clegg Government has also made this channel difficult to access. The aggrieved employee would not have the right to be heard – *locus standi* – if that employee had not followed the internal procedure fully for redress. This Government appears *oblivious* of the dirty tricks of employers or their representatives who would go out of their way to ensure that they obstruct the allegedly-wronged employee from executing all steps of the internal process. This **unreasonableness** of the Cameron/Clegg Government extends to the other two avenues of redress which are the County Court (CC) and the High Court (HC). The time limit for filing in the CC - Sheriff Court (SC) in Scotland - is anytime between three and six months depending on the employment question. The HC allows a conditional grace of six years. These latter two avenues are progressively more expensive to use.

Another major **stumbling** block for the aggrieved employee before s/he can rely on any of the three pathways for redress is the *further* continuation of the unreasonableness of the Cameron/Clegg Government. This is the length of time the employee has to be in service with the employer in question. This *qualifying period* was extended to two years from April 2012 by the Cameron/Clegg Government from its previous one year although certain circumstances would nullify the qualifying period. The Conservative Party, to which Cameron belongs, had previously imposed a two-year qualifying period but was cut to one year by the Blair Labour Government.

So, we have **three** difficulties, which are **principal**, confronting the employee who seeks to take an 'employer' to court for an unlawful employment action. **One** is the first matter of the "qualifying period" in employment to earn the right to litigate. The **other** is whether the employee has exhausted the internal process for redress. **Another** is the issue of financial capacity of the employee to litigate once the right to litigate has been earned – through the qualifying period and exhausting the internal process. As a **first** principle, any mechanisation process of facilitating *fairness* should not be *conditioned* by time limits. What is **unfair** is **unfair** *ad infinitum*. *Justice*, of course, is constrained by, and to, time limits by its very nature. It is a *prescribed* process, and ergo, a *bureaucracy*. *Justice* is one *artificiality* that has to be controlled by another artificiality. As a **second** principle, the facilitation of *fairness* should not be a provision by the same employers who are the subject of the complaint of *unfairness*. There is the possible argument that though the subject of complaint is the employer, the employer might only be the subject of complaint by *vicarious liability*. While this might well be a **factual** argument it cannot be a **justifying** argument for throwing the aggrieved employee back to the wolves. The employer representative or representatives undertaking the review procedure, through *misplaced* loyalty or *misunderstanding* of the real issues at stake, might simply *perpetuate* and *propagate* the grievance of the employee and in doing so **inhumanly** and **inhumanely** stretch the *discomfort* of the wronged employee. As a **third** principle, the *mechanised* process of facilitating *fairness* should not provide **technical** escape routes for an alleged wrongdoer by *financially incapacitating* the alleged victim from instituting claims *for* lack of funds.

The employee, as a litigant-in-person, faces a major *impediment* in the court setting and it is *perennial*. It is not *enshrined* in law but **entrenched** in court practice. It is the **sympathy** of judges for the employer and the **make-belief** that lawyers *are* generally more intelligent than the rest of the population. These court attitudes are demonstrated in a number of ways. (1) Judges have been known to **subvert** the *mechanics* of procedure of court with the arrogant presumption that the litigant-in-person is *unaware* of this *sleight of hand*. Judges grant applications made by employers even when it is clear certain applications are for the purposes of **filibustering**. Such **mindlessness** by judges *unnecessarily* prolongs the duration of the case and judges then *excuse* employer *distortion* of facts with comments such as "it has been a long time and memory fails". Some of these applications, for instance a "stay" of proceedings, are granted the employer even *without* giving the employee litigant-in-person the opportunity to challenge the basis of such applications. It is applying the procedures of "justice" *incorrectly* and arguably *perversely*. (2) Judges have also been known to **misconstrue** the meaning of the law to justify the **lie** that the litigant-in-person is *inadequate* before the lawyer. This *manipulation* of the law assists the **prejudice** of judges in denying victory to the litigant-in-person over a lawyer even where the litigant-in-person had proven **superior** to the lawyer in the *dialectics*. Judges, on occasion, go as far as to *ignore* pertinent facts or *misrepresent* them or *suppress* them *insofar* as having *regard* for those facts would put the lawyer to shame. Once this **dastardly** deed of *eliminating* the facts supporting the employee litigant-in-person is accomplished, British "fairness" makes it impossible to appeal against the **perverseness** of the judge on the basis of this **wilful** abuse of authority.

If the court is the **factual** process it is *pretended* to be, why bestow on Judges the privilege of discretion which they then hide behind to commit their wilful abuse of office? The Court's prerogative "to establish the fact" is not licence to distort and/or ignore and/or suppress fact or facts from one opposing side in favour of the other. It is *extremely* **unethical** in any aspect of human pursuit. In establishing the more *plausible* fact, the intelligent mind will accept all facts presented and *discard* or *regard* them *vis-a-vis* one another on the basis of **reason**. The reasoning for discarding or regarding facts *vis-a-vis* one another should then be **enunciated** in judgments rather than the common practice of *articulating* the strength of facts admitted against the **dismissal** and/or **distortion** and/or **suppression** of **certain** facts of a case. This is **dishonesty** by any *morality* of the human mind.

The entrenched court practices **against** the employee litigant-in-person make it seem as though the courts are in **cahoots** with employers. This is **not** *fairness*. It is **not** even *justice*. In the **true** understanding of the human spirit, it is *power intoxication* in **cowardly** *refuge* behind *justice*. Importantly though, it is **oppression**. It is what Parkin would explain as "*exclusionary closure*".[ix] It is **feudal** that the employee litigant-in-person has gone to court to challenge the *unreasonableness* of the employer but has to contend also with the dishonesty of the court whereas the court is under *legal* **morality** to be **neutral**. The *subversion* of the mechanics of procedure of court and the *misconstruction* are undertaken against the *possible* background of the litigant-in-person being much better educated than either the opposing lawyer or the judge. After all, what is the purpose of education if not to *testify* to one's intellectual acumen? Is the *objective* of education not to set it down **unambiguously** that the higher one's academic qualifications the better one has *powerfully* proven oneself at *understanding* and *interpreting* narratives correctly? For the law profession to argue against the logic of education is to "shoot [itself] in the foot" because one then would ask what the importance of education in law is.

British law-making would argue that the time limits and financial requirements for employment litigation are placed **equally** on both the employee and the employer. It is a **dishonest** argument. Yes, these impositions are placed *pari passu* on both parties but they are not set **fairly**. The employee is an individual with **finite** financial resources and this might bear on that person's ability to litigate within the time limits or litigate at all. The employer, in most cases, is an organisation with more than adequate financial capacity. While British *fairness* would argue that the employer is in court by vicarious liability it refuses to appreciate the logic that the **cause** of that liability is another employee. This employer *incalcitrance* to reason is *simply* mind-boggling. In certain cases, those causes of the employer's vicarious liability, these subject-of-complaint employees are *cowardly* and *scheming* individuals who bank on the *knee-jerk* support of **unlimited** legal resources of the employing organisation.

The alleged abusive employee has the *guarantee* that s/he would not be held *personally* liable for the costs of litigation. This assurance is strengthened by, and in, the *Enterprise and Regulatory Reform Act (ERRA) 2013* which mandates for ET claims "a deposit of up to £1000 as a condition of continuing to advance [a particular] allegation or argument". It is clear that this condition is for and to the *especial* **disadvantage** of aggrieved employees. The principle of this condition as emphasised by Justice Underhill is to "act as a disincentive for claimants to pursue weak elements of cases".[x] Notice that there is no "disincentive" against Respondents submitting "weak elements of" defences. This **legalized inequality** is plain mockery of the British claim of being *fair*.

If the aggrieved employee is able to satisfy the **insensitive** and **unreasonable** stipulations of *ERRA*, s/he still has other *contrived* hurdles to jump. S/he would continue to do battle in the courts with own resources until these resources are exhausted. In the meantime, s/he might not be able to secure another employment simply because s/he is litigating against a previous employer. Yet, Britain prides itself as a *liberal democracy* in which one **member of society** is as *equal* in law, and *protected* in law by the law as another member. A reasonable person recognises from the scenario above of a subject-of-complaint employee **protected** as a *matter of course* by the employer and the aggrieved employee left to **fend** for self by the same employer that it is the subject-of-complaint employee who is protected **de facto** in law by the law. The allegedly abusive-employee is given the right **carte blanche** to play god. It is almost a **de jure** right. This abusive employee is indeed a god where s/he believes s/he has the power to dismiss another employee from employment. Alas, the etiquette of *fairness* within UK consciousness *insofar* as employee-employer disputes are concerned appears premised on the protection of a subject-of-complaint employee.

A *fair* liberal democracy would recognise that where an employee is *prima facie* the cause of the employer's vicarious liability that employee should not be protected by the law *directly* or *indirectly*. Such a **functional** liberal democracy would *enshrine* in law a 'level playing field' for the alleged-against employee and the alleging-employee where both are either supported equally by the employer or are left to fend for themselves in the courts until the outcome of litigation. At the end of the litigation, the losing employee can then pay back to the employer the financial support provided in addition to the costs imposed by the courts (where costs are imposed). The benefit of such a system is *potentially* awesome and it is two-fold. In the **first** instance, it is essentially **tempering** as an overarching condition in employment relations. It will *moderate* the excessive *behaviour* of one employee against the other. An **abusive-employee** would **think** twice about abusive conduct in the work place. Here, I have in mind that employee who, rather than be **sensible** with you, is busy bragging of being your "boss" and your "line manager" and riding roughshod over you in *deed* and in *word*. A **false accuser** employee would also be **wary** of making allegations against colleagues. The abusive staff and the false accuser staff would be very aware that they would have to prosecute their cases from own resources pending the outcome of any litigation. The **thought** of this financial cost would always caution their behaviours in the workplace. In the **second** instance it is **restitutive**. If employee relations went to court and the **truth** prevails, either the subject-of-complaint would be **absolved** of any blame or the aggrieved staff's allegations would be **validated**. Importantly, the *first instance* of **behaviour moderator**, is the **primary** objective of my proposed 'fairness' process. It would stop matters from getting out of hand for reasons of **personal** liability for the **cost** of litigation. The *second instance* of **restitution** could be argued as already taking place within the current *justice* mechanism. However, the proposition would be *preposterous* in *sophistry*. It cannot be said to happen as a **rule** where in the first place we have a number of employees simply 'taking it on the chin' because of the absence of financial resources to prosecute claims. In the second place, there are the occasions of judicial arbiters delivering **perverse** judgments.

British Fairness in Social Policy as an aspect of Law

The **intrinsic** nature of Britain as an *unfair* social organisation is also **explicit** in the award of welfare benefits as demonstrated by (a) housing benefit, and (b) child benefit. Housing benefit is most-closely linked to households not earning an income from the job market. Housing benefit is also associated with households on low income. Child benefit used to be a 'universal benefit', in the sense and practice that all households with children of certain age got it, until the Cameron/Clegg

Government made it an **unimaginable** demonstration of what is **not** *fair* in British society. This Government withdrew the award of the benefit from households where *a* parent earns above a certain threshold a year.

Housing Benefit as Unfair Distribution of A "Collective Consumption Good"

The housing benefit unfair arena revolved around a number of statutes. One is the combination of *Housing Act 1988*, and as amended by *Housing Act 1996*. This establishes how much rent a tenant can owe a private landlord before facing eviction. The other is the *Housing Act 2004* that stipulates the deposit guarantee scheme (*DPS*). Another is the *Welfare Reform Act 2007* that codified Local Housing Allowance (LHA). LHA is given to claimants of welfare benefits renting in the private sector.

The 2007 Act formulated fraudulent behaviour for LHA tenants and the 1988/1996 Acts enshrined in statute protection for this fraudulent conduct. The 2004 Act ensures that the private landlord is penalised most unreasonably on behalf of the tenant. These Acts are *bad* laws individually or collectively. Together, they are **oppressive** laws. They are **thoughtless** laws which infringe upon the human rights of private landlords. These laws question the fundamental nature of *liberal democracy* and *representative democracy* both of which Britain is. It is an issue that examines the *morality* of a Government favouring so blatantly unequally a segment of society to the detriment of another.

The LHA was predicated on the *building-castles-in-the-air* principle by the Blair/Brown Labour Government that it would "foster greater social responsibility" with recipients and somehow teach them how to manage their finances. LHA also allowed recipients to keep up to £15 for themselves if they were able to negotiate that much off their rent. Even at the time of thinking up the idea, its originators must have known it to be **ill-conceived** and was tantamount to patting individuals on the back for not going out there to seek a living, to earn their *keep*, to contribute to the maintenance of their country, to be part of the progressive march of society. Calculating players of the system retained much more than £15 of the LHA. They managed this feat either by winning the sympathy of private landlords or by making false claims to the Department of Work and Pensions (DWP). The Gordon Brown Government later recognised the *stark* unfairness of the £15 LHA gift to claimants that it resolved to remove it in 2009. The removal was deferred to 2011 and it is being removed in stages as required since then.

Certain tenants on LHA also absconded with up to two months' rent without declaring this additional income to the DWP. The non-declaration of the appropriated rent is clearly a breach of the conditions of entitlement to State benefits. It is also theft of funds belonging to the DWP and the private landlord concerned in view of the *Theft Act 1968*. However, the LHA claimant is able to confiscate two months' rent on the basis of the *Housing Act 1988*, and as amended by the **Housing** *Act 1996*. The *Theft Act 1968* and the *Data Protection Act 1998* protect the private landlord but are effective only where the DWP acts responsibly. If the DWP assumes the duty imposed on it by virtue of the *Data Protection Acts* then the private landlord will be able to exercise the right(s) conferred by *Housing Acts 1988-1996*. The Police would also be able to do their job with assistance from the private landlord. The principle of the LHA continues with the Cameron/Clegg Government in the *Universal Credit* scheme.

The unfairness of the *2004 Act* regarding the tenant's deposit has been countervailed to a certain extent by the judgement in *Tiensia v Universal Estates [2010] EWCA Civ 1224]*. It was held in this case that the issue of safeguarding the tenant's deposit by the landlord was strictly one of compliance *per se* and not compliance within the statutory time limit. It was a narrow victory for private landlords. The changes from April 2012 are still weighted heavily against the private landlord. The extension from fourteen (14) days to thirty (30) for the landlord to secure the tenant's deposit does not compare with the tenant's right to owe the landlord circa sixty (60) days rent. Nor is the flexibility (*discretionary power*) to be given to judges to impose a penalty of between one or three times the deposit on a defaulting landlord comparable to no sanction on a defaulting tenant. Besides, to give judges discretionary power to censure landlords within a tariff continuum is to create a breeding ground for **unfettered** unfairness. Importantly, it is **not** reasonable for Government to tell private landlords that being owed rent is a private matter to be pursued in the courts but intervene heavily on the side of tenants when it is the landlord at "fault".

It is worthy that the tenant's deposit is protected from *unpleasant* private landlords. Should the same *morality* not apply that the landlord's rent be protected from a *scheming* private sector, especially the LHA, tenant who knows as much as a lawyer does about the *sanctuary* offered the private sector tenant by the law? The really *nasty* ones can withhold rent for the last two months preceding the expiry of tenancy and damage the property at will. The *most* the private landlord can hope for is a "single claim" with the deposit guarantee scheme and this will *incur* additional financial loss in the fees for the required "statutory declaration". At *best* the *single claim* could only recoup for the landlord one month's rent which is the value of the deposit. The financial *inconvenience* to the private landlord does not stop at making the *single claim*. The landlord has to wait for **fourteen** days *after* departure of the tenant before making the declaration. This waiting period could actually be more than fourteen days if the last day of the waiting period falls on a Friday or the weekend. It then takes the deposit scheme management about **fourteen** days to write to the tenant giving that tenant another **fourteen** days to respond. **Two** months after the eviction of a tenant, the private landlord is still without funds s/he is entitled to by law notwithstanding that the tenant had **absconded** with two months' rent. It is *unfair* law not to appreciate that if a landlord makes a statutory declaration to a deposit scheme, it meant the tenant had not left a forwarding address. If a tenant had not left a forwarding address it is *oppressive* law that does not recognise the tenant would have absconded. It is very *bad* law that refuses to correspondingly expedite release of the deposit to the landlord.

'Universal Child Benefit' as Fairness *and* Unfairness

The 'universal child benefit' represents *fairness* and *unfairness* simultaneously. It is *fairness* in its *distribution* of a **benefit** of society among those who have *contributed* to the **burdens** of society through taxes or other forms. It is *unfairness* in *sharing* a *benefit* of society with those who have *not* borne the *burdens* of society either by paying taxes or giving back to society in kind.

With a condition in the *Welfare Reform Act 2012*, the Cameron/Clegg Government **poisoned** the ***fairness-in-part*** aspect of *universal child benefit* by removing it from households where **a** member *earns* above a specified amount. The operative word is 'earns' (gross - before tax) not 'bring home' (net - after tax) or 'take home' (net - after tax). By the time this gross income is taxed many on welfare benefits could be *better-off* than this hard working household. It is not only *manifestly unfair* but also shows the thinking of *lazy* minds. The consideration to have been engaged when it was decided to remove child benefit from hard working families is so very simple. A reasonable mind would ponder correctly that withdrawing child benefit from a home where one parent earns upwards of the specified amount but leaves it intact for families with combined income above that specified amount because no family member earns above the threshold is **not** a *sane* proposition.

Simple intelligence, that is, intelligence at its *most rudimentary*, would understand that if child benefit were ever thought sensible to remove from working families, such removal should work on the basis of the total income/joint income of that family and not the single highest income of the family. We kept being bombarded with the droning that "the Chancellor needs the money". One would have thought *sensibly* that if the Chancellor **really** does need the money, he would do the intelligent thing and extract the money that he supposedly needs from households with high incomes, combined or single. This is *simple* intelligence. This is intelligence at its *most basic*. At any rate, I am unable to understand what is *fair* about a society that removes child benefit from hard working parents because these parents dedicate their existence to the improvement of their personal circumstances but continues to give it to unemployed parents, certain of whom make the deliberate decision not to work or ever work and have made claiming state benefits a business science, 'a fine art'?

It is **impossible** to appreciate the *fairness* in, and of, the British society that takes away child benefit from parents who recognise that from one's toil one should eat, except for circumstances beyond one's control, but gives it to parents whose attitude to life is the **deliberate** *opposite* in majority cases. Most of the *welfare-benefit fathers* who the Cameron/Clegg Government believe deserving of child benefit are *work-shy*, and who continue to have children with different women at the taxpayers' expense as though it is these fathers' God-given right for taxpayers, the *conscientious* members of society, to care for them and their *irresponsible* conduct. It is a different matter if some high-earning parents decide not to claim their child benefits. *Insofar* as such an action translates into a **satisfying-outcome** for those high-earning parents then the transaction would have been *fair*. I would advise, however, that instead of *declining* to claim the child benefit the better option is to claim it and *donate* it to charity. Importantly, British sense of *fairness* as demonstrated by the Cameron/Clegg Government is to remove child benefit from households with the **natural right** to it, having *shouldered* the burdens of society by paying their taxes and/or contributing usefully to society in some way. *Exemplary* households in British society are **punished** for being exemplary members of society.

Overview of the "Unemployed" Condition

Not all "unemployed" recipients of welfare benefits are "vulnerable" as conveniently argued most of the time by some. The *Church of England* (*CE*) and the *Roman Catholic Church* (*RCC*) with **misplaced** sense of righteousness are especially *culpable* in making this argument. One is *unable* to understand how a person becomes "vulnerable" because that person is unemployed. I was unemployed for many years. My period of unemployment included the time when the unemployed were contributing 20% towards their community charge (the infamous "poll tax"). I did not complain about this community charge because I believed it *fair* that one should not just feed off/on society although I struggled with payments at the beginning. I could not have been considered during this period of unemployment, by any stretch of the imagination, as a **leech** on society. I had a good honours first degree, and somewhat *exemplary* postgraduate qualifications. I had *prepared* myself for "the world of work" and I was more than ready and willing to *engage* work. In addition, I was contributing **in kind** to the Welfare State by giving my time to community organisations in a **volunteering** capacity. My reliance on State benefits was not **conditioned** on vulnerability but on unemployment even though I had and still have sight problems, *inter alia*. I was simply unemployed. Many have argued that if one were unemployed and one were also a drug addict then one could rightly be classified as "vulnerable". I beg to **differ** and differ very strongly. If unemployed individuals become drug addicts it is a **conscious** choice they had made. Nobody would have forced them to take the first step to becoming drug addicts. One might have been cajoled, enticed or even coerced into taking that first step but in the end to take that first step is **voluntary** action.

The *CE* and *RCC* and other apologists of the *misplaced righteousness* see nothing wrong with families dependent on welfare benefits raking in benefit packages of around £100,000 a year for living expenses including living in *palatial* accommodation. They see nothing **unfair** in a man having more than one child either with one woman or with many women **relying** on hardworking taxpayers to take care of him and his family. If his many women live separately, *innocent* taxpayers, as a matter of course, **still** pick up their individual maintenance on benefits. The apologists do not believe it is **unfair** for a woman to have more than one child by a single man or different men but **demands** of *innocent* taxpayers to foot the bill for their upkeep. They consider it *fair* that welfare benefits provide for a person **more** than that person could self-provide were that person in work. For instance, an owner-occupier with a one bedroom property with five children would simply have to do with that property whether or not the children are of different sexes. **Yet**, someone on welfare benefits with the same number of children would expect the State to *provide* housing large enough for the family and the State would, indeed, *oblige*. It does not matter to these apologists that a person on welfare benefits might not have **prepared** in any way for "the world of work". It is *irrelevant* for and/or to these apologists that this person on welfare benefits might not be **bothered** to acquire either academic or vocational *qualifications*. They are not **concerned** that this person on welfare benefits might not care less about **seeking** any form of work related training. It appears not to occur to these apologists that a number of those on welfare benefits place conditions on what work they would do and what they are willing to earn even though they have no qualification - academic or vocational - to justify the conditions they are creating for seeking employment.

I need to make myself clear here about the issue of large families with parents on welfare benefits. I do not see anything wrong with the taxpayer caring for large families where parents had previously contributed to the Welfare State, financially or in kind and had fallen on hard times. I would go as far to say that taxpayers **owe** such families. They are our responsibility because they themselves had not **shirked** their responsibility. I would take a different view though if they continue to add to their large families after they had fallen on hard times. Those large families with parents who have **never** contributed to the Welfare State, financially or in kind, simply **play** the **misguided goodwill** of the Welfare State. I do not believe that the Welfare State should take responsibility for more than one child, under any condition. Individuals with large families living on the Welfare State *simply* cannot continue "eating their cakes" and also "having those cakes". We should be grateful that the Cameron/Clegg Government is putting a stop to the *"play the system"* enterprise by certain claimants of welfare benefits.

Some individuals on welfare benefits continue to impose financial burdens on the taxpayer. Not only has successive Government upon successive Government assured them it is not decent to work. If it is decent to work they would not receive such fabulous State hand-outs. I must **admit** though that the Cameron/Clegg *Welfare Reform Act 2012,* in part, is saying that it is *decent* to work. Certain individuals on welfare benefits pursue the adventure of depriving the taxpayer of possessions the taxpayer has *toiled* blood and sweat for. They perceive encouragement from every sector of the criminal justice system (CJS). If they are not thus encouraged we will not, have light sentencing for property thefts. We would also not have homeowners sent to prison for protecting their homes and their loved ones. Here again, the Cameron/Clegg Government is **emphasising** the homeowner's right to protect her/his property. The taxpayer is forced to contract out for security to the home, the vehicle, and any other tangible possession. If the taxpayer does not secure her/his property in this manner, the offender calls her/him "**stupid**" for the invitation to be relieved of hard-earned possessions. Of course, not all dependants on welfare benefits take up such encouragement. This is why I have used the expressions "certain", and "some". Most would **not** go that far in punishing the taxpayer and this is where George Kelly's work in 1955 *debunks* the rehabilitation school's **unsustainable** insistence that we should examine the offender's background to avoid excessive punishment. I refer them to Kelly's eye-opening work in two volumes on human behaviour. The individual chooses from personal **conditioning** and **preference** how s/he behaves.[xi]

Property Law No Longer Sanctuary for *Unfairness* in British Society

Until the Cameron/Clegg Government, *fair* Britain **legalised** the "adverse possession" of one's property through the *Land Registration Act 1925* and latterly the *Land Registration Act 2002* and the *Limitation Act 1980*. *Adverse possession* is what is commonly referred to as "squatter's right" or "squatters' right". The Cameron/Clegg Government made "squatting" **unambiguously** a criminal offence through the *Legal Aid, Sentencing and Punishment of Offenders Act 2012*. The *Criminal Justice and Public Order Act 1994* already made "squatting" a criminal offence but no State apparatus[xii] was paying attention to this Act *insofar* as it concerned *squatting*. I need to apply some brakes here. There was no such **indulgence** in Scotland because that part of Britain made squatting unlawful by virtue of the *Trespass (Scotland) Act 1865*. This difference again in law between Scotland and the rest of the UK reiterates how very **wrong** to perceive, or even conceive, the UK population as comprising a single *thought-process*, not to talk of a single identity. How very mistaken my Occidental interlocutor was and still is.

Prior to the 2012 Act, squatters **abused** the provision of s.6 of the *Criminal Law Act 1977* with apparent approval from State apparatuses. This Act has been *taken for granted* as criminalising property owners attempting to regain possession of property by force because of the support it renders the *Protection from Eviction Act 1977*. The 1977 Protection Act in s.1(2) criminalises anyone who "unlawfully deprives the residential occupier of any premises of his occupation of the premises or any part thereof, or attempts to do so, ... shall be guilty of an offence ...". The *taken for granted* interpretation of s.6 is **absolute** misunderstanding of its function. The Act was **not** meant for the *indulgence* of squatters but for the **protection** of legitimate occupiers of properties be they owner-occupiers or tenants. By effecting or seeking to effect removal of a squatter from *premises* occupied *unlawfully* without recourse to the Court, a landlord would not be interfering with the squatter's **expropriation** of the said premises. Repeating the same enactment in s.6 of the Criminal Law Act in s.1 of the Protection from Eviction Act confirmed that it was solely for the protection of tenants. It was *clearly* a case of **bad** law making to repeat the same *stipulation* in two separate Statues. While there is to confusion in the minds of *sane* individuals as to what exactly the *stipulation* meant it enabled unscrupulous lawyers to argue *specious* cases and for *resource-wasting* and *time-wasting* Judges to accommodate them. The enactment would have been *sufficient* in the Criminal Law Act alone.

When the Cameron/Clegg Government was embarking on the 2012 Act, even some lawyers were against the enactment of such an Act. They argued that s.7 *Criminal Law Act 1977* sufficiently protected homeowners. These *dissenting* lawyers should go back to learning how to understand the law. For my readers to understand what s.7 of the *Criminal Law Act 1977* says, please find it reproduced here *verbatim*. The most relevant part is s.7(1): "Subject to the following provisions of this section and to section (12A (9) below, any person who is in any premises as a trespasser after having entered as such is guilty of an offence if he fails to leave those premises on being required to do so by or on behalf of - (a) a displaced residential occupier of the premises or (b) an individual who is a protected intending occupier of the premises". The remainder of the section is connected to actions to be taken by all concerned once the Police had done their job.

It is evident that in *statute* this provision protects a residential occupier, and an intending occupier. It does not, however, protect the absent property owner who is neither a residential occupier nor an intending occupier. Importantly, if in practice that section protected home owners as these lawyers insisted why did homeowners; "absent" or a "displaced residential occupier" or a "protected intending occupier" have to *struggle* through the courts and at great expense to reclaim their properties? This is saying much for a *fair* UK (Scotland exempted). A property owner has toiled blood and sweat to acquire property. A trespasser seizes the property, and the rightful owner has to fall into special circumstances before regaining, without use of the civil court, what s/he worked for. How could this possibly be *fair*? The lawful facilitation of the squatter's morally *skewed* preferences imposed substantial financial legal costs on the rightful owner without any legal liability on the squatter. The squatter is allowed to depart the property after damaging the property and/or stealing from it extensively and relying exclusively on taxpayer funding to challenge the rightful owner's right to the property. Yet, the squatter could not have gained access to the property other than by *unlawful* means.

The defence of the trespasser being homeless is *spurious* insofar as it concerns the unlawful possession of premises for the purposes of squatting. In addition, the defence is *nonsense* ordinarily in refusing *simply* to acknowledge that most of the homeless in the UK make themselves "intentionally homeless". Some are homeless because they lose their jobs and consequently their homes. One can understand that. They have not made themselves *intentionally homeless*. Some are homeless because of a relationship breakdown. One can understand this too. They have not made themselves *intentionally homeless*. Most are homeless because they decide to be **itinerant**. This is the category of the majority of the UK homeless. One can understand itinerancy also. It is *human nature* to be itinerant otherwise we would not have left our evolutionary origin of Africa to disperse to the Americas, Asia, Australasia, and Europe. What is not human nature is for us to move from one location to another with the intention **not** to *cultivate* our new environment. If it were human nature to *leech* off our environments, we would not have been able to *evolve* as we have done and/or *build* the great civilizations we had across the world. If humans from the beginning of life had the *squatting* attitude, our species would have been **extinct** by now because we would have **exhausted** what was available that we did not **replenish**.

British Fairness in Discretionary Power to State Apparatuses

'Discretionary Power' given to any State Apparatus in a liberal democracy is an **emblem** of *unfairness*. It is an *anomaly* to the principle of liberal democracy. It is *antithetical* to the value of *fairness*. The British **abode** of *fairness* known as *justice* is **replete** with this **antithesis**. *Justice* is the *playhouse* of the legal exercise of 'discretion'. *Discretionary Power* is privilege and it is **absolutism**, even if it is *temporary* absolutism. It is temporary absolutism because, as always, discretionary power is applied on **ad hoc** basis. Here we remember the English Historian, Baron Dalberg-Acton, with his caution that "... absolute power corrupts absolutely".[xiii] Discretionary Power is *absolute power*.

Rawls maintained that "the basic structure of society is the way in which the main political and social institutions of society fit together into one system of social cooperation".[xiv] The essence of Rawls' proposition here is that the *basic structure* should hold no surprises for anyone. Every member of society understand[xv] what the *basic structure* has in store such as 'a' is 'a' and 'b' is 'b'. *Discretionary Power* throws that *knowing what to expect* out of synchronization ('sync'). *Discretionary Power* **spews** the unexpected and upon the **play of mind** of the one with that privilege. S/he is a god. With *discretionary power* each member of a State Apparatus can apply the process of *justice* on the same issue in very different ways. A police law enforcement officer could stop an individual with a wrap of cannabis and would let that individual go even without a warning. Another police law enforcement officer could stop another individual with a wrap of cannabis but would issue that individual with a caution. Both police personnel would have exercised *discretionary power* but one of them could have been (i) *lenient* on the individual stopped or (ii) *harsh* or (iii) *proportionate*. Importantly, whichever of the foregoing *qualities* is applied, it could have been on the basis of *appearance* and/or *race* and/or *sex* and/or *whim* and/or *any other* reason. Similarly, the same scenarios could take place within a court setting; person 'Y' might receive a more favourable sentencing than person 'Z' for the same offence. This could even be the case if the offence in question was committed under the same circumstances.

The scenarios above *illuminate* exactly why *discretionary power* is the **epitome** of **unfairness**. *Discretionary Power* is **arbitrary** decision making. It is delivering Samuelson's "collective consumption" good in an **impromptu** manner. For Samuelson, "collective consumption goods [or services, we] all enjoy in common in ... that each individual's consumption ... leads to no subtraction from any other individual's consumption ... simultaneously ...".[xvi] To dispense a *collective consumption* good also known as "public good" in an arbitrary manner is not *complimentary* of *fairness* because there is no *standardization* of responses whether as commentary or decision or service provision. Miller recognised this *fallibility* of inconsistencies in law making, for instance, when he argued "... that the penalties for breaking [laws ought to be] standardised, known and applied impartially ...".[xvii] *Discretionary Power* is **condemnation** of natural law, **betrayal** of the principle of liberal democracy, and quite plainly **hazardous** to the *wellbeing* of the populace. It builds *resentment*. Sometimes, the resentment would *bubble* up and *erupt* either in individual or collectively *emission*. This is when we get *eruptions* to civil society.

Other times, the resentment would become *inversed* to the individual and that individual *suffers* a mental breakdown. Yet, others simply resign themselves to this *unfair* state of affairs. Some, however, challenge the *monstrous unfairness* with all the energy they can summon, *every time*, and anyhow but within the confines of *legal* legitimacy, as *moral* legitimacy and *social* legitimacy are not usually embraced by the law.

British Fairness as a Value of the Political Process

I engage the discussion of British *fairness* and *justice* with *clear eyes*. *One*, I am well educated in political philosophy, and a keen scholar of governance practices. *Two*, I have been active within the machinery of "competitive elitism" and I remain a constant observer of the process. *Three*, I was deeply involved for considerable years in community development, that *least* recognised among the many forms of community activism and political empowerment. Thus, I can assure myself that I write with certain authority on the polity of a country that has been my home for *circa* thirty (30) years and which remains my home and to which I have pledged continuing allegiance.

The British system of governance consists of **five** traditions made up of **seven practices**. One; it comprises **three types of democracy**. Two; it is a **constitutional monarchy**. Three; it is **parliamentary oligarchy**. Four, it maintains **hereditary nobility** in its legislature. Five, it appoints **lifetime nobility** (*life peerage*) into its legislature. One democracy is the *procedural democracy* which is the process enabling "the people" to vote professional politicians - Weber's **competitive elitists** - into office.[xviii] The other democracy is *representative democracy* in which *the people* elect the competitive elitists into office to represent the interests of *the people*. Another is *liberal democracy* in which the law is the instrument of managing *the people* in all spheres of activity. The constitutional monarchy is the governing of *the people* with a King or Queen as Head of Government within the confines of a constitution. The parliamentary oligarchy is identified in the circumstance where Parliament **arrogates** to itself in **entirety** the **sovereignty** of *the people*. The arrogators use the exercise of representative democracy to justify their arrogation of the "People's Will" or the "Will of the People". Schumpeter[xix] and Plamenatz[xx] justify this *usurpation* by proposing that the electorate, either by electing representatives or simply by participating in the voting process, has **abdicated** and **renounced** responsibility and **transferred** sovereignty to the elected representatives.

Procedural Democracy and Representative Democracy with the attendant usurpation of the *will of the people* by Parliamentary Oligarchy while beyond the **oversight** of *the people* are subject to **recall** by *the people* through periodic elections but *the people* have neither the **right of oversight** nor the **power of recall** over the constitutional monarchy, the hereditary nobility and appointed nobility. The *will of the people* has no say in who is king or queen or whether there should be a king or a queen in the first place. The *will of the people* cannot challenge the hereditary composition of the legislature nor does the *will of the people* disturb the parliamentary oligarchy that appoints the lifetime nobility. The *will of the people* is argued on two points. One is the assumption that each voting person has leverage equal to one another. In this sense, a *consensus* can always be arrived at through *astute* application of this leverage.[xxi] The result hence is that the individual will benefit immediately from the current decision or defer that benefit, i.e., call in the chips at a later date. The second argument of the *will of the people* proposes that the choices made at various times by the minority allies with those of the majority at varying times. Although I do not buy into these explanations of the *will of the people*, the *will of the people*, as a *generalisation*, is still sustainable.

In *utility*, these identified seven systems of political practice in Britain are, in themselves, **useful** insights into what in the British socio-legal complex is *fair* or *unfair*, and what is *just*. Procedural Democracy and Representative Democracy are examples of the *fairness concept*. Liberal Democracy, Constitutional Monarchy, Parliamentary Oligarchy, Hereditary Nobility and Appointed (lifetime) Nobility are typical of the *justice conception*. It is *fair* that *the people* are given equal opportunities to engage the process of *procedural democracy* in electing representatives of their choice in the spirit of *representative democracy*. These two engagements are as far as *the people* go in the management of their affairs as a body politic. Once in the **Legislature** – *Parliament* in the case of Britain – the *elected* representatives in the *House of Commons* and the *hereditary* representatives and, *appointed* representatives in the *House of Lords* assume the *collective sovereignty* of *the people* as they constitute themselves into the **parliamentary oligarchy**. This parliamentary oligarchy is excused as a *justice* process because these representatives would argue that since they are representatives, they have been given the mandate not to consult *the people* on matters of governance before taking decisions on such matters. Here we find that the notice from Jesus the Christ of "give unto Caesar what is Caesar's" has resonance.

It is the convolution of democracy as I have narrated above and the fallacy of British governance further to my preceding explanation that founded my standing in the 2005 Parliamentary Elections for a London constituency. I stood as a Green Party candidate. Representative Democracy is necessarily **Proxy Democracy** but is not recognised as such. Had I won my seat, I would have introduced *the people* to "direct democracy" by **Particular Proxy** *insofar* as I would be their *constituency* hence **Particular** *spokesperson*. The *will of the people* would always have been triumphant with me as the people's spokesperson in Parliament. I tried again for Prospective Parliamentary Candidate (PPC) selection in the 2010 election through the Tory Party open selection process but received in return a patronising letter that advised me, a seasoned operative in community development across England and Wales, and a competent Politician, to start from scratch.

My political pedigree includes the following. I was a paid up Conservative Party member in 1986, I left in 1988, I think. I then joined the Liberal Democrats circa 1989, I think. I again joined the Tory Party in Hackney in the 1990s and left again. I am politically *sophisticated*. I know what I want. I do not desire position *necessarily*. Interest in political office should not be about **self-aggrandizement**. The pursuit of political office should be motivated solely by the desire to serve *unconditionally*. The competition for political office between **competitive elitists** ought to have basis on the need to correct an error in governance as a legislator or challenge the inadequacy of an incumbent. Success at winning office should come accompanied by the duty to do better than before or better than the *erstwhile* incumbent, and to respect the care-taking responsibility for the *People's Will*. Engagement in political office should seek the harmony of ideas or at the least, some cooperation on ideas beyond partisan politics and across political affiliations. The *fair* way to achieve this *enlightened* way of doing governance is to get rid of the political party institution. Thus, competitive elitists would stand as **independents**. Personal financial resources would not be allowed to play a part where rigid conditions are set on how much a competitor should spend on a campaign. The individuals who wish to stand but do not command the level of the bench-marked funds for campaign should be able to raise the amount from corporate and/or individual supporters. In recent times, Howard Dean showed the world how substantial amount of monies could be raised in dribs from supporters during his primaries for nomination to the Democratic Party ticket for the US presidency. Barack Obama was to confirm the Dean initiative as a *sure thing* with his two successful runs for US President.

Other Titbits of British *Fairness*

It is British *fairness* that every year rail fares are *ratcheted up* above the rate of inflation with no *corresponding* improvement in service provision. We then find rail operators and Government Ministers justifying the *aberration* when neither operators nor ministers pay a penny towards travel on the rail networks. British *fairness* here is privilege for those who contribute nothing towards the maintenance and continuation of something to demand more for the sustenance of that something from those who ensure its continuity. Alas, *fairness* to suggest those "who know it" being the ones "who feel it" is turned upside down in the British context. Those who have earned the right to talk about "it" are shut out.

British *fairness* enables Members of Parliament (MPs) to *advocate* every year for *enhancement* of their salary at a rate considerably above that for other Government employees. Yet, these MPs make bad laws, sleep during important debates or abscond from attending such debates and get to be property magnates by making the taxpayer fund their *multiple* mortgages.

Through British *fairness* we had for decades administrators lording it over medical practitioners in what is called the NHS foundation trust. In some cases these administrators can hardly read and/or write, at least, compared to the doctors and nurses they over-ride. We found one some years ago who claimed to have a university degree but who never leaved through the pages of higher education texts. We again need to thank the Cameron/Clegg for the changes made to this anomaly.

Within British *fairness*, businesses can vary the terms of an existing contract with customers while the customers are denied the options of terminating that contract immediately. Mobile phone contracts are especially subjected to these whims. We know that most businesses operating in Britain, as with other countries, are multinational and/or transnational but they are still bound by the laws of the countries of their individual operations. So, if these multinationals and transnationals short-deal us, it is because our British *fairness* allows them.

With our British *fairness* we experience households as tenants of council properties they are not *entitled* to. In some cases these properties are single properties. In other cases the properties are *multiple*. These council properties are rented out by these *illegal* tenants as their personal properties. Those households become property *magnates* simply from *stealing* State properties. This theft, in turn, deprives those in **actual** need of State housing provision from accessing that provision. So, what is fair about or with council properties stolen for the gain of *unscrupulous* individuals? This instance tells us that we are back in the jungle where the principle is "survival of the fittest" at being criminal by (i) outwitting the *legal* code, (ii) being irresponsive to *social* consciousness, and (iii) being oblivious of *moral* understanding. We are told from this kind of theft that it is okay to appropriate "benefits" from society without sharing society's "burdens". To be *fair* regarding this scenario is to install *efficient* mechanisms to forestall this type of **theft** of State assets.

British *fairness* encourages the *vilification* of lone (single) mothers when their children fall foul of the law. Do these children not have fathers? It is a different thing if a man is not made aware that he is a father. He cannot be chastised for not taking up responsibility he does not know he has. However, in this day and age, if a man is told he is a father, the least he could do is initiate a DNA test if he doubted the woman. This is, if the man is a responsible individual.

As far as *civil liberty* is concerned, British *fairness* stipulates that an individual working with a Police Force cannot report that particular force to the Police Watchdog, the Independent Police Complaints Commission (IPCC) **ordinarily**. This is notwithstanding that the Force in question **prima facie** falls under the conditions for which the IPCC was given its mandate. Importantly, the IPCC is a **lame-duck** organisation; we have case managers who do not have an understanding of the law and/or the guidance to them explaining the law. We know this from the history of the organization. Yet, the IPCC is an organization whose decision the people cannot appeal from. How can this situation be considered a fair process? It is, in reality, a *breeding ground* for the *miscarriage of justice*; the British **recourse** for *fairness*.

Where it matters most, on the issue of "*the defence of the realm*", British *fairness* lost the plot *completely*. There is the immigration rule that **prohibits** British citizens from bringing their non-EU immigrant spouses into the UK unless these citizens earn almost £19,000 per annum. Our Armed Forces personnel are **not** exempt from this policy no matter the policy's credibility. *Fairness* is not a *relative* dispensation between individuals but an **absolute** right of an individual and *particular* to the **conditions** of that individual. It is an 'inalienable right', and **unconditional** at all times. My use of the term 'relative' *semantically* denotes comparison between entities. As the immigration policy is a general rule for the population at large it is *logical* for it to apply to all sections of the population equally. As much as the 'relative' application of the policy is logical, it is not **normatively-logical** as it is applied to our Armed Forces personnel. This is where my use of the term 'absolute' comes in. Not all sections of the population sign a contract of employment to go and **willingly** die for their country or be maimed during service to their country.

Armed Forces Service personnel accept a *death sentence* the moment they join the Armed Forces. They can be deployed to a theatre of war at any time and might not return alive or able-bodied. Any general rule, therefore, for the population ought to make provision for this particular condition of the Armed Forces personnel. Philosophically they are on **borrowed time** until they are discharged from the service and they need to enjoy fully every moment of that borrowed time. An aspect of that enjoyment is to be with those they cherish as much as possible. The blanket application of this immigration rule denies them this enjoyment. British *fairness* does not pay our heroes that much to go die for us but, hey, to enjoy the **happiness** of togetherness with their partners they need to earn up to what we have *decided* not to pay them.

British *fairness* has shown us that when **one** person is in disagreement with **two** persons it is the view of the **one** person that should count. Yet, the British ethic is supposedly based on the *majority principle*. A case of note is the **eventual** "unlawful killing" inquest jury finding in May 2011 over the death of Ian Tomlinson. This jury finding **righted** the **wrong** of imposing the view of one pathologist over the allied view of two pathologists. The wrong was so *perverse*, as that one pathologist whose opinion was preferred over the other two had questions *previously* about his professional competence. If the British are thus *fair* then one should never wish to encounter their *unfairness*.

Conclusion

This essay examines what the British could possibly mean when they say they are "fair and just". It tackles this question by exploring the laws and practices of the British territorial-State. It sets the scene by establishing a durable explanation of *fair/fairness* and a sustainable identification of *just/justice* by visiting the sayings of Jesus the Christ. For *fair/fairness*, he asked us to love the other as we love ourselves and for *just/justice*, he directed that we give to those what they have demanded of us *insofar* as those making the demand have power over us.

Thus, we understand that *fair/fairness* and *just/justice* are parallel values, and one does not mean the other. To be *just* is not *necessarily* to be *fair*. All the illustrated instances in this essay of various absences of *fairness* within the British social milieu are *prescribed processes* of *justice*. We have, therefore, come to recognise *justice* as the *structured mechanism* with which Government manages relations between entities within society whether or not these entities are individuals or a collective of some sort. *Fairness* on the other hand is a *natural* quality of the human being and *latent transactional* expectation between humans. *Fairness* is conditioned by the

precept of '*I will not act towards another person in a way that I would not wish another person to behave towards me*'; *fairness* is really this simple a concept.

We have learnt that being *British* does not bespoke a *homogeneous* identity. The *British* comprises the four main peoples of the English, Northern Irish, Scottish, and Welsh. These four main peoples are *interspersed* with other peoples from Africa, Australasia, Asia, the Americas, Continental Europe, Eastern Europe, and so on.

We have also come to *appreciate* that the British **boast** of custodianship to *fairness* and *justice* pans out *intellectually* as *self-glorification*. We understand this to be *self-indulgence* on *false applause* and *triumphalism* premised on "unconscious falsehood" - the lie that has become the truth such that the liar no longer remembers that the so-called truth is in reality a lie. In reality, this is *hallucinatory* moral consciousness. Thus, the British claim as the conscience of *fairness* and *justice* is the **defend rhetoric** of "false consciousness" – an illusionary appreciation of the *status quo*. It is the **illusionary paradise** of the *ideologue* and as ideologies go, they are either *credible* or *incredulous*.

Endnotes

---

[i]A good way to understand 'rhetoric' is to be familiar with the expression of 'gift of the gab'. Aristotle in 350 BC suggested two types of 'rhetoric' (as well as for 'dialectic'): "Rhetoric is the counterpart of Dialectic. All men make use ... of both ... to defend themselves and to attack others". I have termed the use of 'rhetoric' for defence as the '*defend rhetoric*' and the use of 'rhetoric' for attack as the '*attack rhetoric*'. Please note that someone before me has postulated the notion of '*self-defensive rhetoric/self-defence rhetoric*'. I cannot remember who but I came across this notion in my undergraduate years. The 'rhetoric' does not necessary have a normative logic to it and it is more or less for the purposes of 'rallying cry' (the ideology) whereas the 'dialectic' is normatively logical (but not necessarily acceptable to all). Plato's *Republic* circa 360 BC saw "... rhetoric [as] the art of persuading courts and assemblies; and so, partly by persuasion and partly by force [and] dialectic ... [as] the only science which does away with hypotheses in order to make her ground secure; ..." Note that Aristotle and Plato contradicted each other on the function of dialectics.

[ii]Aristotle., (trans – Ross,W.D.) *Nicomachean Ethics*, Book V, Chapter 2, Batoche Books, 1999. (my emphasis)

[iii]Confucius., (trans – Muller, A.C.) *The Analects of Confucius*, [5:12], 1999/2013, http://www.acmuller.net/con-dao/analects.html.

[iv]Socrates., (narrator - Plato), *Republic*, http://www.idph.net

[v]Ibid.

[vi]Ibid.

[vii]Voloshinov, V.N., *Marxism and the Philosophy of Language*, Mass: Harvard University, 1929. (*Italics in the original*)

[viii]Althusser, L,. *Ideology and Ideological State Apparatuses: Notes towards an Investigation* in Althusser, L., *Lenin and Philosophy and Other Essays*, London: New Left Books, 1977.

[ix]Parkin, F., *Marxism and Class Theory: A Bourgeois Critique*, Columbia: Columbia University Press, 1979.

[x]Department of Business Innovation and Skills., *Employment Tribunal Rules: Review by Justice Underhill - Consultation*, paragraph 63, September 2012.

[xi]See (i) Kelly, G., *The Psychology of Personal Constructs – A Theory of Personality*, New York: Norton, vol.1, 1955, and (ii) *The Psychology of Personal Constructs – Clinical Diagnosis and Psychotherapy*, New York: Norton, vol.2, 1955,

[xii]According to Louis Althusser, 'State Apparatuses' would include such entities as the court, military, police, tax office, *et cetera*. Althusser, L,. *Ideology and Ideological State Apparatuses: Notes towards an Investigation* in Althusser, L., *Lenin and Philosophy and Other Essays*, London: New Left Books, 1977.

[xiii]Dalberg-Acton: letter of April 1887 to Right Reverend Mandell Creighton on opposition to the presumption of "Papal Infallibility".

[xiv]Rawls, J., *Justice as Fairness – A Restatement*, Cambridge, Mass: The Becknap Press of Harvard University Press, 2001.

[xv]'Every' is actually a plural term but has come to dominance as a singular term through bad English.

[xvi]Samuelson, P.A,. "The Pure Theory of Public Expenditure", in *Review of Economics and Statistics*, vol. 36, No.4, (Nov. 1954).

[xvii]Miller, D., *Principles of Social Justice*, 1995, Massachusetts: Harvard University Press.

[xviii]Weber, M., *The Protestant Ethic and the Spirit of Capitalism*, Boston/London: Unwin Hyman, 1930 & Schumpeter, J., *Capitalism, Socialism and Democracy*, London: Allen and Unwin, 1943.

[xix]Schumpeter, op.cit.

[xx]Plamenatz, J., Man and Society – *A Critical Examination of Some Important Social and Political Theories from Machiavelli to Marx*, UK: Longman Group, 1963.

[xxi]Buchanan, James. M. & Tullock, G., *The Calculus of Consent: Logical Foundations of Constitutional Democracy*, Ann Arbor: University of Michigan Press, 1962.